MR. JONES' AUTOGRAPH

If it appears below, this book has become a valuable first edition your heirs will treasure (after they discover it under the leg of that wobbly table you always meant to throw out).

MEDICARE

FOR THE LAZY MAN

2020

SIMPLEST & EASIEST GUIDE EVER!

Copyright 2020 Douglas B. Jones, CLU, RHU

This book and the content herein have been written in order to educate and to simplify a complex subject. Every effort has been made to ensure the accuracy of the content, but there is always room for misunderstanding and misinterpretation. Therefore, no liability is assumed for losses or damages due to the information provided.

The reader is responsible for his own choices, actions and results. He should seek guidance from professionals whenever there is any question as to the advisability of a particular course of action.

WHAT READERS SAY:

Roy Brotherhood

Great how-to guide to Medicare!

I am already on Medicare and did not need this book. I purchased it out of curiosity to see if it took the mystery and fear out of finding a good policy. I was pleasantly surprised to find how well it is written in simple terms and easy to understand.

Typically if you want to find out this information you have to submit your personal/contact information to an insurance company (or agent) and wait for them to call and put the pressure on you to purchase what they offer. This simple book eliminates that hassle completely. While the author offers to assist you, it is your choice to make the contact.

I recommend this book to anyone approaching Medicare age and if you are already on Medicare and want to change your policy this will be an excellent guide to do so.

Leigh Siegel

This is an incredible little book that will guide you through the Medicare process with ease and an incredible sense of humor. I feel so knowledgeable about the subject and I know exactly what I will do when the time comes to enroll.

Thank you Douglas B. Jones

Don't delay! Buy this book today and enjoy! I'm a GTO...

#greatread #medicare #Amazon

Road Warrior

Good things come in small packages

"Don't worry about the book being only 45 pages long. It's worth every penny. The explanation of every Medicare option is concise and helps you to be able to flag a Medicare con man. I've told 3 other people about this book and they all realized they had been sold a bill of goods by an insurance salesperson interested only in a commission. Information in the book also helped them undo a mistake. I'm nearing retirement and after reading the book, am fully confident in whatever decision is finally made regarding Medicare."

Judith R. Riley

"It only took a couple of hours to read, it was funny AND when I was done, I knew what to do.

This short, direct book is a fabulous resource for figuring out the Medicare mystery tour. The author is funny and informative. I had begun researching advantage and supplement plans and was very confused. I asked my older brother what he did about Medicare and he let me borrow this book. I read it, bought my own copy and after reading it felt totally empowered and knowledgeable about what to sign up for when I meet with an agent very soon. You lucky younger people might be able to do it all on-line in the future, check out his website. I'm passing the book on to my younger brother and my friends."

Kathy Fisher

My Insurance Guy Owes Me an Apology

"My insurance guy told me not to bother buying/reading any books about Medicare because they were all stupid. I couldn't resist buying this one because it looked like it might be funny. Well, it also has a serious side and I learned about plan HDF. which is perfect for me. Would my insurance guy have told me about that plan if I hadn't asked him? I'll never know, but he sure was wrong about this book!"

VISIT MY NEW (AND GROWING) WEBSITE!

www.MedicareForTheLazyMan.com

JUST THINK OF THE FUN TO BE HAD!

Buy your Medicare Supplement online

Ask questions

Share complements

Vent frustrations

Join the mailing list

Use the "contact" function to post a manifesto

Tell me what content to add or delete in the 2021 edition

Start a fan club

Study the IRMAA tables

Download government informational booklets:

Medicare & You 2020

Choosing a Medigap Policy: Guide to Health Insurance

For People with Medicare

Revel in thrilling insurance minutia

Be among the first to see the 2021 Medicare pronouncements

Watch a drag race between two 1957 Chevy gassers

Listen to my interview, in which I was cleverly ambushed

Read my highly opinionated blog posts

Join the eager throngs waiting for a podcast episode

E-mail me at www.DBJ@MedicareForTheLazyMan.com

THIS BOOK IS DEDICATED TO: LAZY MEN and the LAZY LADIES who love them, too smart to waste time and energy on stupidity!

It was written expressly for Medicare eligible Americans who:

- Are <u>not</u> infirm, but hope to ensure that **protections** are in place if infirmity strikes.

- Are <u>not</u> destitute, but intend to get **maximum value** from the money spent on Medicare coverages.

- Want to understand **cost effective** ways to defend against catastrophic financial impact of medical treatment.

- Most of all, seek a **simple and clear** explanation of Medicare and the best choices to make.

INTRODUCTION

Why would anyone in their right mind read a book about Medicare?

Never have I seen a subject that causes so much confusion and discomfort for so many people.

In the mid-1960s, the Federal government created this program with the goal of helping older Americans cope with the rapidly rising cost of health insurance. More than half a century later we are saddled with a huge and unwieldy bureaucracy. It confuses the heck out of its intended beneficiaries and has created a class of leaches who fall all over each other in order to profit from that confusion.

Somehow, a giant myth has taken hold of many people approaching Medicare age. This myth holds that:

- Unless one learns about every little aspect of the program, there is a risk of errors.
- These errors will cause disaster and doom that will haunt one for the rest of one's miserable, wretched life.

Who wants to become an expert on all of the ins and outs of Medicare? Why would otherwise normal people decide to waste their time and energy learning about such a mind-numbing subject?

Enter the Medicare "experts" and "advisers"; those who I lovingly referred to above as leaches. These people are generally licensed insurance agents and we are forced to purchase through them because the states have mandated it so.

More than just being licensed, these "experts" and "advisers" have created a belief that only they can guide the helpless through the Medicare morass and into the bright sunshine of eternal happiness and joy. Why would they work so hard to overcome your skepticism and earn your trust?

The Baby Boom!

Those of us born from 1946 to 1964 represent untold riches to the commission-driven leaches in the Medicare advisor community. We are a population cohort that looks like a fat rat passing through a snake. The commissions to be earned by selling us insurance to protect from the flaws and gaps in Medicare constitute a substantial source of income for the average insurance salesperson.

By now you may have realized that I am one of the leaches you are being warned about. I also love to earn commission dollars and I view my fellow Boomers with a certain amount of fiscal lust in my heart. However, the advice I offer to my clients and readers has some major differences from that you will often receive from my fellow leaches:

1) My advice **is much shorter and much easier to grasp.**
2) My advice **may offer a bigger bang from the bucks you spend.**
3) My advice **will allow you to tell your agent exactly what you intend to purchase (and why).**

Studying all of the minutia about Medicare is a huge waste of time and effort.... unless you enjoy that sort of thing of course. Why?

Because knowledge does NOT equal power! Nothing you memorize about Medicare will allow you to improve it in order to get better or cheaper protection. Also, any implication that disaster will ensue if your Medicare selections are not absolutely perfect is equally false.

In reality, very few Medicare decisions are completely irrevocable; mistakes and poor choices can usually be fixed within a year or less. In fact, the costliest mistakes actually stem from refusal to act, as in the case of late enrollment penalties.

One more thing: In prior editions of this series all of my secret advice was located in Chapter 1. Readers often tore out those pages and threw away the rest of the book (harder to do with the Audible or Kindle versions). Eventually, I came to the realization that my primary retail marketing company was offering potential readers a free look at the first 20 pages without having to actually buy the book. Those pages included a distillation of my super-secret advice plus many of my best jokes.

I will no longer try to sell a cow while my retail partner gives away the milk for free. The important substance of my thinking is now deeper in the book.

<u>CHAPTER 13 contains the short version of everything the average reader needs to do with regard to Medicare enrollment.</u>

It may be the only chapter of this or any other Medicare book you actually need to read.

NOMENCLATURE: <u>PARTS</u> vs. <u>PLANS</u>

Original Medicare consisted of two elements called **<u>PARTS</u>:**

<u>PART A</u> – *covers inpatient treatment in a hospital or skilled nursing facility*

<u>PART B</u> – *covers outpatient treatment in doctors' offices, etc.*

<u>Added to the Medicare program more recently are:</u>

<u>PART C</u> – *So called "Advantage Plans" which I do not recommend*

<u>PART D</u> – *Prescription Drug Plans (PDP) defray the cost of drugs*

<u>Coverages that supplement Medicare are called **PLANS**:</u>

MEDICARE SUPPLEMENT <u>PLANS</u> – *protect against the gaps in Medicare*

PRESCRIPTION DRUG <u>PLANS</u> – *PDPs which defray the cost of drugs*

<u>*IN THIS BOOK I ONLY DISCUSS*</u>:

MEDICARE <u>PART A</u>
MEDICARE <u>PART B</u>
MEDICARE SUPPLEMENT <u>PLANS</u>
PRESCRIPTION DRUG <u>PLANS</u>

<u>*These four provide the best protection available.*</u>

CONTENTS

ABOUT THE AUTHOR

Douglas B. Jones, CLU, RHU

Medicare snuck up on me just as it does with most Americans.

As a long-time health insurance professional, I was expected by friends and clients to be ahead of the curve. Turns out I needed to educate myself on this complex subject in order to be able to offer solid advice.

After graduation from the University of Arizona I joined my family's John Hancock insurance agency in Chicago's Loop. Even though life insurance sales with the John Hancock was a 3-generation family calling, I found more satisfaction in helping clients with their health insurance needs.

Eventually the company stopped offering those products so I left to pursue my mission with other companies.

Decades later at a social event, I was asked by several people for a short version of my Medicare advice. They assumed I must be an expert since we were all rapidly approaching age 65.

That was the catalyst that convinced me to learn what Medicare was all about. After a period of study, I formed some conclusions that are directly at odds with other Medicare advisors.

One evening a couple of longtime friends came over to act as my Guinea pigs. The wife, ever the serious student, was lugging all of the printed material they had received and expected me to educate them on every one of the Medicare options available in our area.

The husband was mostly interested in the beer I offered. His opinion was that this whole Medicare decision process was an unpleasant inconvenience that should end quickly.

Very soon, these friends had a complete grasp of my best Medicare advice and the reasons behind it. They were stunned that the whole thing could be boiled down to such a simple conclusion. As they discovered, the most time-consuming part of the process was completing the insurance paperwork.

That evening set the pattern for virtually all of my subsequent encounters with Medicare eligible citizens. Years later it occurred to me that the same process could be offered to everyone in the country who was staring down the barrel of Medicare.

Thus was born Medicare for the Lazy Man!

CHAPTER 1

How may I help you?

For what reason have you decided to buy (or shoplift) this book?

- Are you closing in on Medicare age?
- Considering leaving job-related insurance coverage?
- Responsible for advising a friend or relative?
- Reexamining the choices you made years ago?
- Suffering from insomnia?
- Paying the price for a dissolute life?

Are you seeking a quick and painless guide through the Medicare maze?

What is your destination?

Until I dragged her out west to the University of Arizona, my wife attended a Catholic grade school and Jr. High, a Catholic girl's academy and a Catholic Women's college.

Eventually I realized that Catholic schools do not teach geography because she cannot navigate her way out of a wet paper bag.

However, after reading this very simple road map and following my suggestions, you will have found an easy route to your goal of selecting and acquiring the essential layers of coverage necessary for protection under Medicare:

MEDICARE PART A
MEDICARE PART B
MEDICARE SUPPLEMENT PLANS
PRESCRIPTION DRUG PLANS

That is all you need for complete protection, and it is very likely that these coverages will serve you well for the many decades of life you have yet to enjoy. There will be no need to do an annual review or renewal for anything except perhaps the Prescription Drug Plan (PDP) and then only if you want to make sure your costs are still the absolute lowest possible.

The purpose of this book is simplification of a complex subject.

If that simplification is successful it should relieve the angst many feel when the time comes to make decisions about Medicare coverage.

Among these pages the average citizen confronting Medicare for the first time will discover a short, direct path from start to finish that will relieve their concerns and likely save them some money.

Notice I said "average citizen". The recommendations in this book are not for everyone, but the target audience includes the majority of those approaching Medicare eligibility.

My book has been written for those with:

Average or better health

Average or better financial resources

No desire to waste time or effort studying Medicare

Most helped will be people responsible for their own health insurance, specifically those about to turn 65 and employed people contemplating retirement or termination from an employer's health insurance plan.

Those who are destitute or stricken with debilitating medical conditions should drop this book and seek advice from their state's

Medicaid (welfare) office as well as insurance agents in their immediate locale. Most areas of the US have "special needs plans" locally available and designed specifically for people in dire straits.

Once again, **if you are infirm or destitute, stop reading right now and try to get a refund. This book is not for you!**

CHAPTER 2
What the heck does Medicare do?

If you spent some of the 1960s within range of WLS-AM 890, Chicago's 50,000-watt rock blowtorch, you probably heard the legend of a very lazy young guy named Hootie Sapperticker. DJ Art Roberts promoted June 22 as Hootie Sapperticker Day, but the campaign never really gained traction and Hootie eventually faded into obscurity.

Decades later, Hootie and the Mrs. turned age 65 and, with my guidance, signed up for Medicare through the government on its "oh so user-friendly" website.

Because they learned that Medicare coverage is full of gaps and flaws, they also purchased insurance to protect themselves from those weaknesses in the program - insurance to supplement Medicare known as a **Medicare Supplement.** Clever, huh?

As luck would have it, Mr. & Mrs. Sapperticker have a cute little grandchild who spends part of every day in a bubbling germ factory known as nursery school. After enjoying hugs and kisses from this grandchild, they each contracted a major dose of the most contagious flu of the season. Surviving this disease required visits to a hospital ER, admission for inpatient treatment and some follow-up appointments with the family doctor after being released from confinement.

Hooty Sapperticker expected massive medical bills to start arriving shortly after treatment, but that did not happen. Because they are protected by Medicare, the invoices from the hospital, the doctors, the laboratory etc. were all sent to the federal government for payment. That process started as the patients showed their ID cards to office staff when treatment began.

After calculating and paying their share, the government functionaries (in the guise of Medicare) sent notification to the insurance company that issued their Medicare Supplement policies. The clerks at the insurance company double-checked the government calculations and then issued checks to the providers of medical treatment for the balances due them.

Months after their full recovery, the financial consequences of their illness were resolved. The very conservative Mrs. Sapperticker had purchased the Cadillac of all Medicare supplement plans and paid a monthly premium of around $150. She was delighted to find that her medical bills were paid in full – 100% coverage.

On the other hand, Hooty has always been more of a risk-taking party animal. He had purchased the high-performance Pontiac GTO of Medicare supplement plans for about $50 per month. Hooty had to write checks for a few hundred dollars in cost sharing because of the deductible his plan carries, but this was more than offset by the $100+ he saves each month in lower premiums. In addition, his beer funds have been protected from bill collectors.

The happy conclusion is that I, as the Sapperticker family insurance advisor, have been elevated to heroic status and toasted in absentia every time they gather together.

The cute little grandchild was never told about all of the misery caused by his grandparents' unconditional love.

SO, WHAT IS THE BIG DEAL ABOUT MEDICARE, ANYWAY?

Now that we understand **Medicare is a simple bill paying mechanism** for those Americans it covers, why is there such a hoo-rah about it?

Hapless citizens in their middle sixties are accosted with piles of insurance company propaganda and endless warnings about the dangers of charging into Medicare without professional guidance. Commission-driven leaches who promote themselves as "experts" are always happy to foster confusion that leaves customers vulnerable to their guidance. Other, more altruistic advisors have opined that responsible citizens must spend hours absorbing junk mail, Medicare-related textbooks and other scholarly tomes. They have also suggested attending educational seminars and meeting with government officials in their offices. The implication is that you risk financial disaster and eternal damnation if you do not study and memorize all aspects of the Medicare morass.

This is a complete load!

It is really all about the commissions, folks!

This is why you will be buried in pitches for Medicare Advantage plans that have the richest commission schedules, followed by smaller piles of come-ons for Medicare Supplement plans that have less generous commission schedules by which insurance agents are paid.

However, you will never be told about my favorite plan, the best kept secret in Medicare. In order to force a discussion about the plan I most often recommend, you will have to grab the typical agent by the lapels and say the magic words: **high deductible.**

More about this closely guarded secret later in the book.

CHAPTER 3
Medicare Part A

Your goal in buying, borrowing or stealing this book should be to minimize the time and effort required to establish your Medicare related coverages. Let's get to it!

MEDICARE PART A is health insurance provided by the Federal government. It is intended to reimburse some or all of the expenses incurred during treatment in an inpatient facility (hospital, skilled nursing and rehabilitation).

In almost all cases, Americans with a 10-year work history (or those married to someone with a 10-year history of taxable employment) will have Part A provided to them free of charge.

Since it is free, almost everyone is advised to enroll in Part A coincident with their 65th birthday.

That coverage effective date (as with all Medicare-related coverages) will be on the first of the month in question.

Generally, someone turning 65 may enroll up to three months before the birthday month begins. Coverage will then go into effect on the 1st day of that birthday month. They also have a few months available to enroll after the birth month, but this might mean going without coverage for some period.

- Exception: if the actual date of birth is on the 1st of any month, coverages will become effective on the 1st day of the prior month.

    Don't ask why this is so; nobody knows.

- Exception: if the existing health insurance plan is an HSA (Health Savings Account) and you would like to continue making pre-tax contributions, it might be wise to consult an expert about delaying enrollment as coverage by Part A may preclude deductible HSA plan contributions.

ENROLL IN MEDICARE PART A ONLINE HERE:

https://www.ssa.gov/medicare/

The enrollment process may possibly take as few as 10 minutes.

CHAPTER 4
Medicare Part B

At the risk of belaboring the obvious, the following is my official definition of the second part of Medicare:

MEDICARE PART B is health insurance provided by the Federal government. It is generally intended to reimburse expenses incurred during treatment by doctors in an outpatient setting as well as testing & diagnostics, medical equipment, supplies and preventive care.

It is very important to choose the effective date of your Part B coverage carefully. Medicare Part B carries a substantial monthly premium (starting at $144.60/month in 2020) so it would not be prudent to start it too early.

More importantly, since Medicare Part B is critically important protection designed to reimburse the costs of the most commonly encountered treatment, it would REALLY not be prudent to enroll too late.

Late enrollment for Part B, after becoming eligible, risks incurring hefty medical expenses without insurance protection. If one fails to enroll until after the eligibility period, the opportunity to enroll will be limited to a short period at the beginning of each following year and coverage will not become effective for several months after that.

In addition, substantially late enrollment in Part B subjects one to a lifetime monetary penalty that will be added to the monthly premium forever.

The importance of timely Part B enrollment cannot be stated too strongly.

Turning age 65:

Medicare eligible people who are responsible for their own health insurance will have no difficulty choosing an enrollment date. They will turn age 65 and will properly enroll with an effective date of the first day of their 65th birth month.

- Exception: if the actual date of birth is on the 1st of any month, coverage will become effective on the 1st day of the **prior** month.

  Don't ask why this is so; nobody knows.

The enrollment period begins 3 months before the birth month, and prudence dictates that the enrollment process should begin as early as practical within that 90-day period.

Retirement from a group medical plan after turning 65:

Medicare coverages should be scheduled to begin when the group plan terminates. It is not prudent to have any gap in coverage and it is really bad to have a gap lasting longer than 63 continuous days. At that point your medical history might come into play as to when you will be allowed to have full coverage for all medical conditions.

Before starting the enrollment process, download Form CMS-L564 from the internet and have your employer's HR people complete their portion. This will verify that you were covered as an active employee in the company medical plan until your termination date.

Other circumstances that might affect your coverage decisions:

- Do you have a spouse who is actively employed?
- Are you not a US citizen?
- Are you on COBRA or retiree medical coverage from an employer group plan?
- Are you eligible for Tricare or other VA coverage?
- Do you fall into another category that complicates things?

If any of the above apply, you may need professional advice about whether, or exactly when to begin Medicare Part B coverage. You should seek that advice from any of the unbiased sources I have listed **below.**

ENROLL IN MEDICARE PART B ONLINE HERE:

https://www.ssa.gov/medicare/

The enrollment process may take as few as 10 minutes.

Some unbiased sources of information and advice on choosing the proper Medicare effective date for you/your spouse

Helpful contacts in each state

www.Medicare.gov/contacts

SSA: The Social Security Administration (which administers the Medicare program)

https://www.ssa.gov/medicare/

Choosing a Medigap Policy: A Guide to Health Insurance for People with Medicare:

https://www.medicare.gov/pubs/pdf/02110-medicare-medigap-guide.pdf

Public service agencies, like a local hospital for instance, may have a Medicare and Social Security advisor on staff.

Your company HR department

Medicare & You 2020:

https://www.medicare.gov/sites/default/files/2019-09/10050-medicare-and-you.pdf

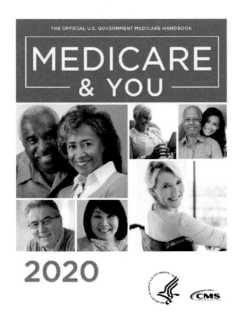

Medicare for Dummies Cheat Sheet

http://www.dummies.com/personal-finance/insurance/health-insurance/medicare-for-dummies-cheat-sheet/

SHIP – State Health Insurance Assistance Programs – choose your state from the drop-down menu

SHIPTACENTER.org

CHAPTER 5

Medicare Is Not Enough Protection!

If you have started the Medicare enrollment process with plenty of time to spare before the effective or starting date, of your coverage, take a break. Do something more fun or productive until your Medicare ID card arrives.

Eventually, you will receive the new Medicare ID card in the mail. It will show your unique alpha/numeric "identifier" and the start dates for Parts A and B.

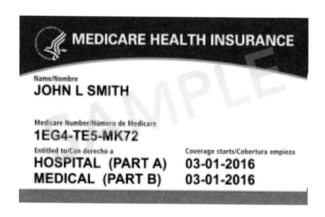

Now is the time to purchase the insurance that will protect you from the dangerous gaping holes in Medicare protection.

What are these gaping holes you ask? They are the deductibles, coinsurance, co-pays and unlimited lifetime cost sharing amounts that severely limit the protection afforded by original Medicare.

These cost sharing elements of Medicare Part A and Part B have no statutory limit. Potentially, very large amounts of money are at risk for people on Medicare who have not purchased additional protection from a private insurance company. Someone once calculated that, if everything that could go wrong did go wrong over $900,000 in medical expenses could be charged to a Medicare participant who was only covered by original Medicare.

Insurance to supplement Medicare

Two basic types of insurance are available to protect you from financial disaster. One is clearly superior.

1. **MEDICARE SUPPLEMENT PLANS** – The best and only choice for health insurance to supplement Medicare, assuming you can afford a modest monthly premium cost.

Medicare supplement plans range from very comprehensive to very cost effective. In keeping with my goal of simplification, I have only recommended the very rich Plan F or the streamlined High Deductible Plan F (HDF). People who are first Medicare eligible in 2020 have a different choice to make.

If you are a youngster who will not be eligible for Medicare until 2020, the simplest and most comprehensive supplement plan available to you will be Plan G. The most cost-effective plan you will be allowed to purchase will be the brand-new High Deductible Plan G (HDG). Information about HDG has been slow in coming from the insurance companies who say they intend to offer it to their customers.

MEDICARE SUPPLEMENTS GIVE YOU FREEDOM!

Read the next two chapters (6 & 7) to learn why I only recommend Medicare supplements to all of my clients.

2. **MEDICARE ADVANTAGE PLANS (PART C)** – Do not even consider these or waste your time learning about them.

This type of supplemental coverage actually removes Medicare Parts A & B, along with all of their benefits and protections. Original Medicare is replaced by an insurance company plan that forces participants into an HMO-like gulag of rules, regulations and restrictions. The only reason you hear about Medicare Advantage plans so often is that they pay very generous commissions to the insurance agent – thanks in large part to you, the American taxpayer.

You can read more about Medicare Advantage (Part C) in Chapter 8 if you have some time to kill.

CHAPTER 6

Medicare Supplement Plans– The ONLY Way to Fly!

When compared with the highly-flawed Medicare Advantage (Part C) plans, Medicare supplement plans have only one disadvantage: they are not given away free of charge.

Each Medicare supplement plan has a monthly premium charge, although the costs vary widely between states, insurance carriers and type of plan.

The available plans are standardized from company to company and each is denoted by a letter. So, as an example, Plan A provides the same protections and benefits no matter which company sells it.

There are twelve Medicare Supplement plans being sold to Medicare eligibles and they all have one great thing in common:

COMPLETE FREEDOM OF CHOICE!

1) Medicare supplement plans **never have restrictive networks of doctors and hospitals**. A person covered by a Medicare supplement plan is free to seek treatment from any provider who accepts Medicare payment. The greatest medical specialists in the world practice in various facilities around the

United States and none of them have been placed out of reach by an arbitrary insurance company network list enforcer.

2) No network means no **lists to consult when it comes to figuring out what providers to use, no risk of nasty surprises** when seeking treatment away from home or in an emergency situation.

3) A patient covered by a Medicare supplement may **seek treatment from any specialist anywhere without requesting permission** from a gate-keeper.

4) Medicare supplement plans, just like Medicare Parts A & B, are **good anywhere in the 50 US states and possessions**. The plans I recommend also have a $50,000 lifetime benefit for emergency treatment in foreign countries.

5) Medicare supplements are guaranteed renewable and will provide the same level of benefits forever, just as long as premiums continue to be paid. The onset of critical illness will not cause the coverage to be changed or terminated. The insurance company must live up to all of its obligations but the policy holder's only obligation is to continue payments when due.

6) A cautionary note: After your initial period of guaranteed issue eligibility, insurance companies may question your medical

history if you apply for a different plan or to a different company. My advice is to choose your insurance carrier and your supplement plan very carefully because you just may have that plan for the rest of your life.

How does one decide which of the twelve Medicare supplement plans to purchase?

Follow my recommendation to buy either the luxurious Cadillac or the high-performance Pontiac of Medicare supplement plans.

LOTS OF BANG FOR A REASONABLE AMOUNT OF BUCKS!

Two Medicare supplement plans I recommend for the average consumer:

The most comprehensive coverage allowed by law; **the luxurious Cadillac of Medicare supplements**:

PLAN G – for those turning 65 in 2020;
PLAN F – for those who are older.

-OR -

Great protection at an exceedingly low price; **the high-performance Pontiac GTO of Medicare Supplements**:

HIGH DEDUCTIBLE PLAN G – for those turning 65 in 2020;
HIGH DEDUCTIBLE PLAN F – for those who are older.

Each of these Medicare supplement plans covers **100%** of the following costs (except the Part B deductible as noted), filling in the many gaps in original Medicare:

Part A deductible
Part A coinsurance and hospital costs
(up to an additional 365 days after Medicare benefits are used up)
Part A hospice care coinsurance or copayment

Part B deductible – NOT covered by Plan G
Part B coinsurance or copayment

Part B excess charges

Skilled nursing facility coinsurance

Blood (first 3 pints)

AND:
80% of foreign travel emergency expenses after a small deductible
(up to a $50,000 lifetime total)

PLAN F has no deductibles, co-pays, co-insurance nor any other cost sharing provisions. The insured person will not receive any invoices for routine cost sharing expenses. You cannot buy this plan if you became eligible for Medicare in 2020 or later.
PLAN G will reimburse everything but the Part B deductible ($198 in 2020).
HDF and **HDG** credit the above expenses to their deductibles until they are met, and then pay at 100% for the rest of the year.

Here is more about my favorite Medicare Supplement plans. The simplest is **High Deductible Plan F**, which those eligible before 2020 may continue to buy. Newest is **High Deductible Plan G** which will be available to all eligibles as soon as insurance companies kill enough trees to print up all of their legal descriptions and disclaimers. All I know is that it will have the same deductible as HDF and that it most likely will not credit the Part B deductible to offset part of the plan deductible.

Both of the high deductible plans are saddled with an unfortunate and scary name. The insured will NOT have to pay the first $2,340 of medical expenses, only the much smaller Part A or Part B deductibles, depending on the type of medical treatment they must have. After that, if the treatment continues, Medicare pays the vast majority of the expenses while the High Deductible plan applies the smaller unpaid segment of the expenses to its deductible, leaving the practitioners to send invoices for those relatively small amounts to the insured. The insured typically has been saving as much as $100 per month by not buying an expensive Plan F or G, so kicking in a few bucks here and there still leaves him with plenty of lettuce in his wallet.

Unless one is thrown into a hospital, these small invoices will be for 20% of the outpatient charges considered to be Medicare Part B expenses. Part B has an annual $198 deductible (in 2020) and then a 20% coinsurance for Part B treatment costs so individuals covered by the high deductible plans will pay 20% of their charges out-of-pocket in exchange for saving substantial premium dollars.

I illustrate in Chapter 7 that the term **"high deductible" is a complete misnomer**, since Medicare pays benefits no matter what supplement plan – if any – is in place.

CHAPTER 7

The best kept secret in Medicare: High Deductible plans!

High deductible plans are a terrific bargain! Too bad most agents won't talk about them. You see, they would rather earn hefty commissions than to give valuable advice that might cut into their earnings and save the client some money. The fact is, agents earn more when the product they sell is more costly!

The official description of these plans is that they have a hefty $2,340 "annual deductible" before picking up the balance of all unpaid medical bills. This completely ignores the fact that Medicare will begin paying the bills right after its very small deductible has been covered.

The insured **WILL NOT PAY THE FIRST $2,340** of medical bills if they get sick or hurt! Medicare will pay the lion's share of the bills after the relatively small Part A/Part B deductibles (depending on the kind of treatment needed). The insured will pay a much smaller percentage of the bills until, in the unlikely event of a very bad year, his small portion adds up to the plan deductible. After that – 100% baby!

The name "high deductible" is completely misleading and the downside risk is so very limited that the average person will be flush with extra cash from the first month after buying the HD plan! The reality is that Medicare will have been paying 80% of outpatient expenses starting right after that $198 deductible!

Do you remember the beautiful days before Obamacare changed the health insurance landscape, driving up costs and removing many of the choices people could make? Most people had a medical plan that imposed a small deductible first, then a co-insurance or cost sharing period and finally began to pick up 100% of medical bills for the rest of the year. For instance, a common plan could be described as having a $250 deductible, 80/20% co-insurance of the next $5000 and 100% thereafter. This was almost universal until a few years ago and did a good job of protecting people from otherwise painful medical bills.

A smart Medicare Supplement purchaser may keep a similar level of protection, and at a very small monthly premium charge. A person buying the High Deductible Plans F or G will have something like a $200 deductible, then 80/20% of the next $10,000 and then 100% coverage for the rest of the year.

MEDICARE WILL ALWAYS PAY ITS PORTION FIRST. Medicare doesn't know whether there is a supplement or not, it just goes along paying its 80% of the outpatient bills (after the $198 deductible). For Part A expenses, it pays all of the hospital charges after the $1,408 (per admission) deductible. This means Medicare pays 100% of hospital costs after a reasonable deductible and 80% coverage for outpatient expenses after a small deductible, even if there is no supplement in place. In the unlikely occurrence of a disastrous series of medical events, the downside risk of High Deductible plans is very reasonable indeed.

As stated elsewhere, this book is written with a particular audience in mind: those who are not infirm and those who are not destitute. This group can generally afford to pay the reasonable price of regular Plans F or G, the Cadillac and most popular of Medicare supplement plans. However, as comprehensive as the benefits of F and G are, they may not be the most cost-effective choice.

My healthy clients always appreciate the cost/benefit of High Deductible plans once it is properly explained to them that the term "HIGH DEDUCTIBLE" is a complete misnomer. When we are talking about outpatient Part B expenses, what we really have is a $198 deductible and 20% coinsurance of the next $10,000. After that the plan pays 100% for the rest of the year.

It is extremely unlikely that the average person will have total bills anywhere near $10,000. That means he will be saving somewhere near $100 per month year after year by choosing a High Deductible plan. So, in a good year, the policy owner will likely save $1200 or more in comparison to the higher cost of Plan F or even Plan G.

What if disaster strikes and medical expenses grow to a very large number in a given year? The insured person has plenty of downside protection from nasty surprises. If he has to spend all of that $2340 out of pocket towards the deductible and coinsurance, remember that he very likely saved $1200 in premium costs so that leaves just under $1200 (or about $100 per month on the average) to meet his share until the High Deductible plan starts paying 100% for the rest of the year.

What about the monthly savings the insured enjoyed for the many years that expensive medical treatment was not needed? ...and what about the many years of good health and monthly savings that will follow that one unfortunate year?

MONEY IN THE BANK!

CHAPTER 8

Medicare Advantage (Part C) Plans: Why Not?

The only advantage I can see in Medicare Advantage plans is that they don't cost very much to buy. In fact, many of them have $0 monthly premiums! Good deal, right?

Sure, they can be a pretty good deal if nothing bad happens to you; no serious injury or illness that causes the need for medical treatment. In other words, you will be just fine with a Medicare Advantage plan until you actually need to use it.

Insurance agents love these plans because of the generous commissions they pay (thanks to the largess of the taxpayers). Why should you, the insurance buyer beware the hidden booby-traps in Medicare Advantage plans? Where are the flaws in Medicare Advantage or Part C plans for the potential customers like you?

The big one: **NO FREEDOM OF CHOICE!**

1) MEDICARE ADVANTAGE (Part C) plans are HMOs or PPOs. They all rely on networks of physicians and hospitals to deliver care. This adds the complication of having to choose your provider from a list of names to ensure treatment will be covered.

2) One must do comparison shopping every year because the networks are constantly in flux, with some doctors quitting and others joining. If your favorite doctor were to quit your network, you would be stuck finding a replacement from the list given to you by the insurance company. Plans that include drug coverage will often change their formularies, sometimes rendering the whole plan a great deal more expensive.

3) The average Advantage plan has an out-of-pocket limit of over $5000 per year with some having a limit as high as $6700. Why would someone be uncomfortable with a High Deductible plan out-of-pocket limit of $2300 by comparison to that much higher possible loss?

4) Even the most highly touted Advantage plans can beat an insured to death with hidden fees and co-pays. One best selling plan in Florida has co-pays like this: ambulance: $300; hospital stay: $175 per day for first 10 days; diabetic supplies: 20% coinsurance; diagnostic radiology: up to $125 co-pay; lab services: $100 per day; outpatient X-rays: up to $100 per day; therapeutic radiology: $35 up to 20% co-pay; renal dialysis: 20% of the actual fee.

5) Costly complications can spring out of the bushes to cause unpleasant surprises. For example, your surgeon might

belong to the network but the anesthesiologist he uses may not; the radiologist may be in the network but the specialists who interpret the films may not be. In these examples, you should expect to receive a hefty invoice in the mail.

6) Frequently, permission is required prior to seeking consultation with a specialist.

7) Networks often operate in localized areas and traveling out of it or living in a second home somewhere can be a problem, if medical treatment is needed.

8) They will promise that out-of-network emergency care is covered, but may balk at cooperating when it comes to paying for it.

9) Insurance agents who try to enroll hapless victims into a "low cost" or "free" Advantage plan will then sometimes badger them to purchase additional Hospital Indemnity insurance to pay the hidden expenses not covered by the Advantage plan.

10) The many extras they tout, like dental, vision and hearing coverage are often disappointing limited benefit discount plans rather than true insurance coverage. In addition, they

rely on small networks of doctors and dentists, further restricting freedom of choice.

SOMETIMES WE GET WHAT WE PAY FOR!

How can an insurance company give away a product for free? This only works if the government pays the freight. When the government decides to cut its expenses, the insured clients will be the ones to pick up the slack. In the meantime, very large commissions mean that you will never cease hearing about the wonderful world of Medicare Advantage from insurance agents.

The good news is that holders of Medicare Advantage (Part C) plans are allowed to switch from one plan or company to another every year during AEP or Open Enrollment, which allows dissatisfied subscribers to try out a new plan to be effective the following January 1st.

Have you noticed that there is a huge amount of direct mail, TV ads, internet pop-ups and other annoying insurance talk happening every fall? This is because the poor saps who found themselves stuck with Medicare Advantage plans have an opportunity to try something else…. anything else to replace the crapola they bought last year.

Once again, **I do not recommend these plans** for my audience of Medicare eligibles who are not destitute or infirm.

CHAPTER 9

Drugs? We Don't Need No Stinkin' Drugs!

PDP, Prescription Drug Plan or Part D – buy it ASAP!

In their infinite generosity, the Feds now subsidize the cost of prescription drug plans that can be purchased from private insurance companies. Each of these companies can price their drug plans where they want to, compile their own list of drugs to be covered (formularies) and offer different levels of benefit to their customers.

Here are the problems: the construction of each drug plan sounds very complicated to the non-insurance professional; there are deductibles, co-pays, co-insurance and a big scary donut hole to contend with.

Additionally, the formularies and premiums can change from one year to the next and each individual's prescription medication requirements can change.

Therefore, I recommend comparing all available plans only on the basis of the estimated out of pocket cost per year. If the changes in formulary, premium cost or drug needs warrant, the insured can select a new company and a new plan during the annual open enrollment period for the following year.

There is a fairly painless way to compare the cost of all of the drug plans in your locality via the government website. Look for the easy navigation directions below.

What if you are so healthy that you take no prescription drugs at all? After thanking the ancestors who passed down your particular gene pool, consider whether there might be a need for insuring against high prescription costs anytime in the future. If not, and you expect to never, ever purchase one of these drug plans, you are finished right now.

On the other hand, most people without crystal balls like to keep their options open and hedge their bets. And they generally want to avoid the lifetime late enrollment penalty.

If a person becomes eligible to purchase a PDP but elects not to do that, and then decides to go ahead and buy one sometime in the future, a late enrollment penalty will be assessed for each month elapsed from the initial eligibility period to the actual purchase.

The penalty amounts to roughly 35 cents per month for each month elapsed. That means an extra $4.20 per month for a one-year delay, $8.40 per month for a two-year delay, $12.60 per month for a three-year delay and so on.

This is why I advise my clients to buy an inexpensive PDP (maybe $13 per month) when they are first eligible, even if they take no drugs yet.

Admittedly, not all have followed my advice, but I sleep better at night knowing that I tried.

Kind of like child rearing.

EASY NAVIGATION INSTRUCTIONS TO SELECT THE LOWEST COST PDP:

Go to this site: https://www.medicare.gov/plan-compare

click: "**continue without logging in**" (simplest for the casual user)

- Creating an account & logging in here allows your drug list to be retained for future use

click: "**Drug Plan (Part D)**"

Enter your ZIP code and click: "**Select Your Location**"

click: "**I don't get help from any of these programs**"

click: "**Yes**" (you want to see your drug costs when you compare plans)

Select your preferred way of filling prescriptions (retail drug store, mail order or both)

Add your prescription drugs: start by typing the first drug on your list, then click "**Add Drug**" when it turns green.

Add information about each prescription drug on your list. Be sure to click the green button **"Add Drug to My List"** before starting each new entry.

click: **"Done Adding Drugs"** after all prescription drugs have been listed

Select 1 to 3 of your favorite drug stores, even if you only plan to use mail order. Click **"Done".**

Next page lists all available PDPs in your area. Default sort on upper right side is "**Lowest monthly premium**".

- **CRITICAL**: Change to **"Lowest Drug + Premium Cost"** using drop-down menu.

Observe the list of all available plans arranged in order of total annual cost from lowest to highest.

Click **"Add to compare"** on 2 or 3 plans and then click **"Compare"** to be taken to the comparison page.

Make a decision as to which plan you want to purchase. I advise using total annual cost as the basis for that decision.

Click green **"Enroll"** button to buy the new plan.

Cancellation of your existing PDP will be automatic once your application to the new plan has been accepted

Remember that at each AEP in the fall subscribers will be allowed to change to another PDP if they wish.

After completing this process, you will be presented with a thorough comparison of the annual costs for both retail and mail order purchase of the drugs on your list. I advise ignoring the figures for monthly premium, deductible, etc. Your objective is to find the plan that will give you the **lowest total annual cost**, based on your current prescription needs and favorite places to have those prescriptions filled.

If you were successful in following the directions, the least expensive plan will be at the top of the list. You may then use the "Enroll" button to contact and enroll online in your chosen PDP.

Consider repeating this process next year at the Annual Enrollment Period (AEP) in the fall to ensure you have the lowest cost plan.

CHAPTER 10
What Will All of This Cost?

There is a monetary cost for all insurance coverage and government supplied health insurance is no exception. The good news is that, if you are coming off an Obamacare type of plan, the new costs will look like a bargain to you!

A note about IRMAA – the success penalty. This stands for Income Related Monthly Adjustment Amount and may add to the monthly premium for Medicare Part B and for the Prescription Drug Plan, based on what the IRS has recorded as your MAGI (Modified Adjusted Gross Income) two years ago.

IRMAA tables generally change each year. For this reason and the limitations of book publication, please look for the current IRMAA tables on my website, MedicareForTheLazyMan.com. You will find tables there for the IRMAA penalties related to both Medicare Part B and the Prescription Drug Plan.

The target audience for this book is likely to encounter the following monthly premium costs in 2019:

Medicare Part A
    Free of Charge (after 40 quarters of taxable earnings)

Medicare Part B

$144.60 (IRMAA could increase it substantially)

Medicare Supplement Plans: Premiums vary widely depending on several factors.

These include state of residence, age, sex, ZIP code and sometimes smoking status

HIGH DEDUCTIBLE PLAN F –

most cost effective – estimated between $30 and $80

HIGH DEDUCTIBLE PLAN G –

not yet available

PLAN F –

most comprehensive - estimated between $140 & $250

PLAN G -

generally less than Plan F because Part B deductible is not covered

PDP –

Prescription Drug Plans - $13.00 and up, depending on plan and location plus drug deductibles, co-pay and co-insurance.
PDP premiums are also subject to an IRMAA penalty assessment; consult the PDP IRMAA table on MedicareForTheLazyMan.com.

2020 MEDICARE COST SHARING PROVISIONS

PART A - Deductible and co-insurance payable by you or your Supplement

> Deductible per <u>hospital admission</u> = You pay $1,408
>
> Co-insurance hospital days 1 to 60 = You pay $0
>
> Co-insurance days 61 to 90 = You pay $352 per day
>
> Co-insurance for lifetime reserve days 91 to 150 = You pay $704 per day
>
> <u>Skilled Nursing Facility</u>:
>
> Co-insurance days 0 to 20 = You pay $0
>
> Co-insurance days 21 to 100 = You pay $176 per day

PART B

> Annual Deductible = $198
>
> Co-insurance (no limit) = 20%

CHAPTER 11

Massachusetts, Minnesota & Wisconsin

The three states addressed here somehow managed to persuade the Federal Government to grant waivers allowing them to create their own Medicare Supplement plans. All of the general characteristics that make supplements superior to Advantage plans still apply to these outliers. For example, they all work anywhere in the United States and they have no restrictive doctor or hospital networks.

Otherwise, the benefit structure of these state designed plans differs markedly from the Medicare Supplement plans we have discussed that are available in the other 47. The following descriptions are drawn, in part, from www.medicare.gov. To peruse the actual coverage details, go to that site and search "Medigap-in-(state)".

MASSACHUSETTS

The Bay State has two plans available, named "Core Plan" and "Supplement 1 Plan". Each of them includes the same set of Basic Benefits plus additional elements that fill the gaps in Original Medicare plus some state mandated benefits. The bottom line is that the Core Plan is lean and probably much less costly than the Supplement 1 Plan.

Want to save money? Obviously, the Core Plan is going to be less expensive than the Supplement 1 Plan, no matter which insurance company is offering them. The only strategy I can see is to carefully examine the additional benefits covered by the Supplement 1 Plan to decide for yourself if the savings in premium dollars by purchasing only the Core Plan would be worth the risk. As an example, you may not plan to travel abroad, or you have no expectation of being committed to a mental hospital. These are coverages you likely can avoid paying for without concern.

MINNESOTA

In the North Star State there is a plethora of Medicare Supplement plans available for sale: Basic; Basic plus a selection of optional riders; Extended Basic and Medicare plans High Deductible F, K, L, M, and N. There is also set of Basic Benefits common to the Basic and Extended Basic plans.

The optional riders and other choices are interesting and may allow one to create a Medicare Supplement that would cover every possible risk. However, my advice for healthy people seeking great protection at a very attractive cost would be to carefully consider High Deductible Plan F.

WISCONSIN

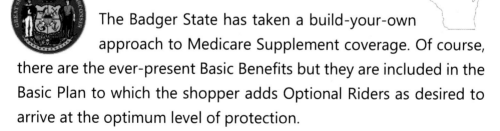

The Badger State has taken a build-your-own approach to Medicare Supplement coverage. Of course, there are the ever-present Basic Benefits but they are included in the Basic Plan to which the shopper adds Optional Riders as desired to arrive at the optimum level of protection.

The benefit description also mentions the existence of a High Deductible plan with a $2000 deductible. If the pricing has been calculated as most similar plans have been, this would offer the most bang for a very few bucks!

CHAPTER 12

Did You Make A Boo-Boo?

It is very likely that you are hearing about the excellent benefits of Medicare Supplement plans and especially the great cost advantage of HIGH DEDUCTIBLE PLANS F & G (HDF and HDG) for the first time.

Since commissions payable to agents are more substantial for Medicare Advantage plans, those are the ones that are promoted most vigorously to the unsuspecting public.

Is that the case with you?

Were you kept in the dark about Medicare Supplements and High Deductible plans?

Are you anxious to make a change so that you can enjoy the benefits of Medicare Supplement plans along with all of my happy clients?

Well, I have good news and bad news for you:

GOOD NEWS: You may apply for a Medicare Supplement policy from an insurance carrier any time the mood strikes!

BAD NEWS: There is no "guaranteed issue" period for Medicare Supplement plans after your initial enrollment period when you first became eligible. You MAY be asked a series of questions about your medical history in order to prove that you are insurable.

This is not true in every instance or in every state but generally you will have to jump through some hoops in order to be allowed to buy a Medicare supplement policy outside of the initial enrollment period. You might be refused if your medical condition and history do not meet the insurance company's insurability standards.

There are a few special exceptions but understanding them and the related complexities is what makes Medicare so much fun.

My website may be able to help, depending on where you live: www.MedicareForTheLazyMan.com

CONTACT ME:

DBJ@MedicareForTheLazyMan.com

CHAPTER 13

POSSIBLY THE ONLY PART OF THIS BOOK YOU WILL NEED!

Are you in charge of your own health insurance and hoping to simplify the Medicare coverage selection process?

The next few pages will allow you to ignore the prevailing confusion and purchase the best, most comprehensive medical insurance available.

STEP 1.

Have you selected your Medicare Part A start date? (Read more in Chapter 3)

Have you selected your Medicare Part B start date? (Read more in Chapter 4)

ENROLL IN MEDICARE ONLINE HERE:
https://www.ssa.gov/medicare/

The enrollment process could take as little as 10 minutes.

Only two more steps to go!

STEP 2.

Contact a licensed insurance agent and apply for your Medicare supplement plan.

Coverage should be effective on the same date as your Medicare Part B.

What follows are descriptions of the two types of Medicare supplement plans I recommend and sell:

CHOOSE YOUR MEDICARE SUPPLEMENT PLAN

LUXURIOUS CADILLAC OF MEDICARE SUPPLEMENT PLANS – most comprehensive coverage

Best suited for those with comfortable finances, low risk tolerance and desiring 100% coverage no matter the cost.

PLAN F: The most popular choice and only available to those already on Medicare (or who would have been eligible for Medicare before 2020 by virtue of age or disability). This has generally the highest monthly premium but has the richest benefit structure. PLAN F pays 100% of all deductibles, co-pays and co-insurance. The insured will not receive any invoices for cost sharing expenses when all medical treatment is Medicare approved.

PLAN G: Set to become the most popular choice and certainly the richest benefit structure after PLAN F. Pays all of the expenses listed above except for the annual $198 Part B deductible. This is the simplest and richest plan available to those first becoming eligible for Medicare in 2020 or later.

 HIGH PERFORMANCE PONTIAC GTO OF MEDICARE SUPPLEMENT PLANS – most cost-effective coverage.
Best suited for those having somewhat higher risk tolerance, willing to accept some limited cost sharing expenses in return for a substantially lower monthly premium cost.

HIGH DEDUCTIBLE PLAN F: Covers all of the risks of legitimate expenses as are covered by PLAN F above. However, instead of paying at 100% from day one of each year, it pays at something less than 100% with the insured making up the relatively small difference. In the unlikely event of very high medical expenses, the plan starts paying 100% after the insured's portion adds up to $2,340 (in 2020). Substantially lower monthly premium than PLAN F, but is not available to those becoming eligible for Medicare in 2020 or later.

HIGH DEDUCTIBLE PLAN G: Details of this brand-new plan have not yet been publicized so anything I say is speculation. It probably will have the same annual deductible as **HDF** above but should cost even less because the $198 Part B deductible will not be a covered charge.

STEP 3.

Select the least expensive Prescription Drug Plan (PDP) from a list of all plans available in your ZIP code.

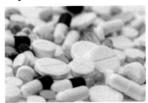

Purchase that plan online directly from the insurance company.

Below you will find step-by-step navigation instructions leading you to that list of PDP plans arranged in order of annual cost.

These instructions look complicated, but it is a government website and so was not designed to be user-friendly. The most complicated part of the process will be entering the detail for each of your current prescription medications.

Since the PDPs are one-year contracts, annual costs can change at the discretion of each insurance company. Also, your prescription drug needs may change during the course of the year.

Therefore, you may find this a worthwhile project to do each year during the Annual Election Period (AEP) in the fall, in case you would like to buy a new plan for the following year.

EASY NAVIGATION INSTRUCTIONS TO SELECT AND PURCHASE A LOW COST PDP

Go to this site: https://www.medicare.gov/plan-compare

click: **"continue without logging in"** (this is simplest for the casual user)

- Creating an account here allows your drug list to be retained on the site for future use

click: **"Drug Plan (Part D)"**

Enter your ZIP code and click: **"Select Your Location"**

click: **"I don't get help from any of these programs"**

click: **"Yes"** (you want to see your drug costs when you compare plans)

Select your preferred way of filling prescriptions (retail drug store, mail order or both)

Add your prescription drugs: start by typing the first drug on your list, then click **"Add Drug"** when it turns green.

Add information about each prescription drug on your list. Be sure to click the green button **"Add Drug to My List"** before starting each new entry.

click: **"Done Adding Drugs"** after all prescription drugs have been listed

Select 1 to 3 of your favorite drug stores, even if you only plan to use mail order. Click **"Done"**.

Next page lists all available PDPs in your area. Default sort on upper right side is "**Lowest monthly premium**".

- **CRITICAL**: Change to "**Lowest Drug + Premium Cost**" using drop-down menu.

Observe the list of all available plans arranged in order of total annual cost from lowest to highest.

Click "**Add to compare**" on 2 or 3 plans and then click "**Compare**" to be taken to the comparison page.

Make a decision as to which plan you want to purchase. I advise using total annual cost as the basis for that decision.

Click green "**Enroll**" button to buy the new plan.

Cancellation of your existing PDP will be automatic once your application to the new plan has been accepted

Remember that at each AEP in the fall subscribers will be allowed to change to another PDP if they wish.

.

If you were successful, CONGRATULATIONS! Your Medicare

prescription drug plan (PDP) work is done!

Furthermore, if you were able to complete all three of these steps, you now have acquired the four essential elements of protection:

MEDICARE PART A
 MEDICARE PART B
  MEDICARE SUPPLEMENT PLANS
   PRESCRIPTION DRUG PLANS

ACKNOWLEDGMENTS

This book would not exist. I would still be sitting at my desk with fingers poised over the keys and eyes caressing the mountains around our Arizona home were it not for my wife.

Mary is among my most rabid critics but can often be brought around to my way of thinking with some persistent persuasion. Once on my team, she is an invaluable asset and a source of insight, inspiration, motivation and support.

Mary is not really high maintenance, but she does need to be reminded periodically that "spousal unit" is actually a term of loving endearment. Not much else to say after almost 50 years of partnership and teamwork.

Thanks to my personal clients who helped me form the idea for this project after realizing why they were all so frustrated.

Others, generally without being pestered, have explained complicated technological mysteries, prodded me out of lethargy or sharpened red pencils to gleefully perform surgery on my sterling prose.

They have shared companionship, cocktails, encouragement, ribald jokes and philosophical pontification, all without ever a negative word about this relatively ambitious project. So I also thank, in no particular order:

Randy & Margaret Carson of C2C Consulting, LLC	Brian and Teri Jones
Paul and Kathleen Bowling	Gerry and Lisa Schafer
Roy and Kathy Brotherhood	Tony and Melisa Coletto

Finally, for no reason other than I just enjoy them, I must acknowledge the youngest generation of my gene pool.
Thanks for making the rest of us proud and happy to have you in our family:

Max Coletto & Alex Coletto -
        Californians just starting to spread their wings.

Drew McMillin, Robbie McMillin and Kate McMillin –
        Canadian-Americans proud to wave both flags!